SPEED MACHINES

CORVETTE

Julia J. Quinlan

PowerKiDS
press

New York

Published in 2013 by The Rosen Publishing Group, Inc.
29 East 21st Street, New York, NY 10010

First Edition

Editor: Jennifer Way
Book Design: Greg Tucker

Photo Credits: Cover Stephen Mcsweeny/Shutterstock.com; pp. 4–5 Rod Beverley/Shutterstock.com; p. 6 Hulton Archive/Archive Photos/Getty Images; pp. 7, 21 Brad Remy/Shutterstock.com; p. 8 Barry Blackburn/Shutterstock.com; p. 9 Steffen Foerster Photography/Shutterstock.com; pp. 10–11 © Hans Dieter Seufer/c/age fotostock; pp. 12, 14 Bryn Lennon/Getty Images; p. 13 AMA/Shutterstock.com; p. 15 Clive Rose/Getty Images; pp. 16, 18 Car Culture/Getty Images; p. 17 (top) Gary Whitton/Shutterstock.com; p. 17 (right) Raymond Boyd/Michael Ochs Archives/Getty Images; pp. 19, 20 Maxim Blinkov/Shutterstock.com; pp. 22–23 Stephen Hew/Shutterstock.com; p. 24 breezeart.us/Shutterstock.com; p. 25 Dongliu/Shutterstock.com; p. 26 Neil Balderson/Shutterstock.com; p. 27 Darrell Ingham/Getty Images; pp. 28–29 Boykov/Shutterstock.com.

Library of Congress Cataloging-in-Publication Data

Quinlan, Julia J.
  Corvette / by Julia J. Quinlan. — 1st ed.
     p. cm. — (Speed machines)
  Includes index.
  ISBN 978-1-4488-7460-6 (library binding) — ISBN 978-1-4488-7532-0 (pbk.) —
  ISBN 978-1-4488-7607-5 (6-pack)
  1. Corvette automobile—Juvenile literature. I. Title.
  TL215.C6Q56 2013
  629.222'2—dc23
                          2012005991

Manufactured in the United States of America

CPSIA Compliance Information: Batch #B4S12PK: For Further Information contact Rosen Publishing, New York, New York at 1-800-237-9932

Contents

American Power

The Chevrolet Corvette is an American classic. Its design was inspired by European sports cars, but it remains true to its American roots. The Corvette was made to **compete** with and beat European sports cars on the racetrack. Corvettes are built to be high-performance cars, but they are **produced** in ways that keep them more **affordable** than many European sports cars, such as Ferraris and Porsches. Its cool design and great performance combined with its affordability give the Corvette a wide appeal.

The first Corvette was made in 1953, and Corvettes have been in **production** ever since. It is the American sports car that has been produced the longest. Since 1953, the Corvette has established itself as a leader in the sports-car market and has sold more than 1.5 million cars.

People are always excited to see the latest Corvettes at a car show.

Chevrolet Cars

Chevrolet, which is a **division** of General Motors, makes the Corvette. Louis Chevrolet and William C. Durant founded Chevrolet in 1911. They wanted their company to compete with Ford and its new car, the Model T. In 1915, Chevrolet introduced its first model that could truly compete with the Model T. It was called the Chevrolet Model 490. It cost $490, which was $5 less than the Model T cost. In 1918, Chevrolet joined General Motors.

Here is Harley Earl with a 1950 Buick LeSabre. Earl was a designer for General Motors and known for creating eye-catching cars, which included early Corvettes.

Corvettes were designed to be the American version of European sports cars.

The first Corvette came out in 1953. It was a white convertible with a red interior. Harley Earl was one of the people behind the design of the Corvette. Before Harley Earl, people did not give much thought to the overall design of American cars because people thought that American car buyers cared more about how well the car worked. Earl knew that in order to compete with European sports cars, the Corvette had to be eye-catching and stylish.

Powerful Engines

The Corvette is known for its **innovation**. That means that over the years, it has been updated with the latest technology and design. These changes have kept Corvettes among the fastest, most powerful, and stylish cars on the road.

Corvettes have V8 engines. This engine gets its name from the fact that the engine has eight **cylinders**, which are laid out in a V formation. The more cylinders an

Corvettes have long fronts and short back ends and sit very low to the ground. Shown here is a Corvette Z06.

The Corvette Z06 has a General Motors LS7 V8 engine, shown here.

engine has, the more powerful it is. Non-sports cars often have only four or six cylinders. Having eight cylinders makes the engine roar as the driver **accelerates**.

The Corvette is also known for having the option for a convertible top. The first Corvette was a convertible, and all of the current models have that option.

9

Corvette Sports Cars

In 2012, there were six different models of Corvettes being produced. They are the Coupe, Convertible, Grand Sport Coupe, Grand Sport Convertible, Z06, and the ZR1. Even though most Corvettes cost less than half of what European sports cars such as Ferraris cost, they are just as powerful under the hood. For example, four of the six current Corvette models have 430 **horsepower**. Horsepower is the unit used to measure engine power. The other two models have even more power. The 2012 Z06 has 505 horsepower and the 2012 ZR1 has 638 horsepower!

The 2012 Corvette Coupe has a top speed of 190 miles per hour (306 km/h). The Z06 has a top speed of 198 miles per hour (319 km/h), and the ZR1 has a top speed of 205 miles per hour (330 km/h)!

The sixth-generation Z06 has been in production since 2006.

Winning Racecars

Chevrolet makes special models of the Corvette to be driven in races. These cars are not made for everyday driving. In fact, it is illegal to drive them on regular roads. The most recent Corvette racecar is the C6.R. The C6.R GT1 was introduced in 2005 and was replaced by the C6.R GT2 in 2009. Corvette Racing, the team that races Corvettes, still races an earlier model called the C5-R. The

The C5-R racecar, shown here, was based on the fifth-generation Corvette.

The C6.R racecar, shown here, is based on the sixth-generation Corvette Z06.

C5-R was introduced in 1999. It has been very successful. It has even beaten the Ferrari racecar in several races!

The 2004 model of the C5-R had a 6.98-liter V8 engine. It had a six-speed manual **transmission** and weighed 2,511 pounds (1,139 kg)! In 2010, Chevrolet introduced the C6.R GT2. It was based on the ZR1 sports car. The GT2 has 485 horsepower and a 5.5-liter engine.

Endurance Racers

Corvettes compete in grand tourer, or GT, races. The Corvettes used in these races are specially made to be racecars. They are much faster and more powerful than regular sports cars. One of the race series that Corvette Racing competes in is the American Le Mans Series, or the ALMS. Corvette Racing has competed in the ALMS since 1960. ALMS holds both sprint races and long-distance races. Corvette Racing competes in the long-distance races. Corvette Racing finished sixth in the 2011 ALMS race held in Long Beach, California.

Here is a Corvette C5-R in an endurance race called 24 Hours of Le Mans.

Corvette Racing's cars are built by Pratt & Miller, which is one of General Motors' official racecar manufacturers.

Corvettes have also been driven as pace cars in National Association for Stock Car Auto Racing, or NASCAR, races. The pace car does not actually race, it is a **symbolic** position. It goes around the track with the racecars and pulls off before they start racing.

First Generation

The first Corvette was made in 1953. It was a white convertible that had a red interior. Only 300 of this first model were made. The 1953 convertible was not a powerful car. It was made for cruising, with a 150-horsepower, six-cylinder engine. In 1956, Corvettes changed from cruising cars to racing-inspired cars. The V6 engine was replaced with a V8 engine. The Corvette's horsepower increased, as did its top speed. Chevrolet also increased the Corvette's production. In 1960, production topped 10,000.

The 1957 Corvette was the first model to have a **fuel-injected** engine. Fuel-injected engines work more efficiently than the **carburetor** engines earlier

Here is a 1960 Corvette. Harley Earl chose to make the car's body out of a material called fiberglass. Chevrolet was the first big car company to use this new, light material in car bodies.

1957 Corvette

Engine size	4.6 liters
Number of cylinders	8
Transmission	Manual (stick shift) or automatic
Gearbox	2 speeds (automatic), 3 or 4 speeds (manual)
0–60 mph (0–97 km/h)	6 seconds
Top speed	132 mph (212 km/h)

Above: Here is a 1957 Corvette, which was the first year that a fuel-injected engine was available for the car.
Right: This 1953 Corvette was one of only 300 that were produced. Although it was not a powerful car, its beautiful design helped establish the Corvette brand.

Corvettes had. All modern cars use fuel-injected engines. Before the 1957 model, Corvettes had three-speed manual transmissions or two-speed automatic transmissions. The 1957 model offered the option of a four-speed transmission. The first generation of Corvettes ended in 1962.

Second Generation

The second generation of Corvettes began in 1963. The Corvettes made during this time, from 1963 until 1967, were also called Sting Rays. The 1963 Sting Ray was available both as a coupe, or hardtop, and as a convertible. The 1963 Sting Ray was also the first Corvette to have split rear windows. The second-generation Corvette's body was designed to be more **aerodynamic** than the models of the first generation. "Aerodynamic" means that air flows around the car without slowing it down much. The force of air slowing down a car is called drag. Designers used a wind tunnel to design and test the aerodynamic shape of the car.

Here you can see the split rear window on a 1963 Corvette Sting Ray.

1963 Sting Ray

Engine size	5.35 liters
Number of cylinders	8
Transmission	Manual or automatic
Gearbox	2 speeds (automatic), 3 or 4 speeds (manual)
0–60 mph (0–97 km/h)	6.1 seconds
Top speed	132 mph (212 km/h)

Here is a 1966 Corvette. *Automobile* magazine named the second-generation Corvette number one on its 100 Coolest Cars list.

The 1963 model was very popular. It was so popular that Chevrolet had trouble keeping up with demand. At one point, there was a two-month waiting list to get one! Altogether, 21,513 of the 1963 Corvette Sting Ray were made.

Third Generation

The third generation of Corvettes lasted from 1968 until 1982. This time period saw a lot of changes in the car industry. For the first time, carmakers began thinking about how much gas their cars were using and how much pollution they were letting out. This was because people realized that they needed to be kinder to the **environment**. Chevrolet made some changes to the Corvette that made it slightly less powerful.

This 1970 Corvette Stingray convertible has its top pulled up. Here you can see the long-nosed shape for which Corvettes became known.

1968 Stingray

Engine size	5.4 liters
Number of cylinders	8
Transmission	Manual or automatic
Gearbox	2 speeds (automatic), 3 or 4 speeds (manual)
0–60 mph (0–97 km/h)	6.5 seconds
Top speed	128 mph (206 km/h)

The hoods on many cars open at the front, but a Corvette's opens at the back of the hood. The car shown here is a 1978 model.

The third generation of Corvettes was called Stingrays, rather than Sting Rays. The 1968 Stingray was heavier than previous models and had a slightly thicker-looking body. This new shape of the car became Corvette's signature look from then on. It had a long nose and a small back. Just like the previous generation, the third-generation Corvette was available either as a coupe or as a convertible.

Fourth and Fifth Generations

The fourth generation of Corvettes was produced from 1984 until 1996, and the fifth generation was made from 1997 until 2004. In this 20-year period, there were many changes and innovations to the Corvette. Horsepower increased from 205 in 1984 to 405 in 2004! At the beginning of the fifth generation, the Corvette was redesigned to include all of the best available technology. The 1997 Corvette was **modernized** and made more driver friendly but with greater power and speed. The 1997 Corvette had a top speed of 172 miles per hour (277 km/h). It could go from 0 to 60 miles per hour (0–97 km/h) in just 4.7 seconds.

The fourth and fifth generations of Corvettes offered a smoother ride with easier, better handling. The interiors were also made roomier. This made these cars more comfortable for both the drivers and the passengers.

The fifth-generation Corvette Z06 was produced from 2001 until 2004.

1997 Corvette

Engine size	5.7 liters
Number of cylinders	8
Transmission	Manual or automatic
Gearbox	4 speeds (automatic) or 6 speeds (manual)
0–60 mph (0–97 km/h)	4.7 seconds
Top speed	172 mph (277 km/h)

Sixth Generation

The sixth generation of Corvettes began in 2005. These modern Corvettes are very powerful and very fast. They are made to be as powerful as possible while still being street legal. "Street legal" means that the car is made to be driven on regular roads and not racetracks. In 2008, Chevrolet introduced the 2009 Corvette ZR1. The ZR1 was the first Corvette that could truly compete with European sports cars in terms of speed and power.

Here is a 2009 ZR1. When this car was still in the planning stages at General Motors, it had the code name Blue Devil.

2012 ZR1

Engine size	6.2 liters
Number of cylinders	8
Transmission	Manual
Gearbox	6 speeds
0–60 mph (0–97 km/h)	3.4 seconds
Top speed	205 mph (330 km/h)

One of the differences between fifth-generation and sixth-generation Corvettes is the headlights. New Corvettes have exposed headlights, while older models had covered ones.

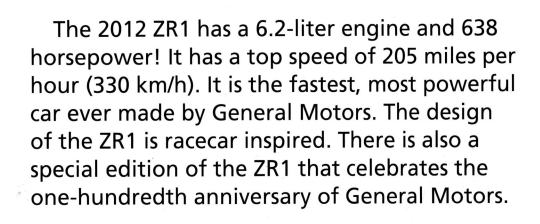

The 2012 ZR1 has a 6.2-liter engine and 638 horsepower! It has a top speed of 205 miles per hour (330 km/h). It is the fastest, most powerful car ever made by General Motors. The design of the ZR1 is racecar inspired. There is also a special edition of the ZR1 that celebrates the one-hundredth anniversary of General Motors.

C6.R GT2

In 2010, Chevrolet introduced the newest Corvette racecar, the C6.R GT2. Chevrolet wanted there to be a strong link between Corvette sports cars and racecars, so it based the GT2 on the ZR1 sports car. The GT2 has a similar body design to that of the ZR1. Both cars have the same steering system and windshield. They also have the same aerodynamic shape. The GT2 has a V8 engine, just like the ZR1. The GT2 has to meet different requirements from the ZR1, though. It must be very safe. Because racecars go so fast, it is easier

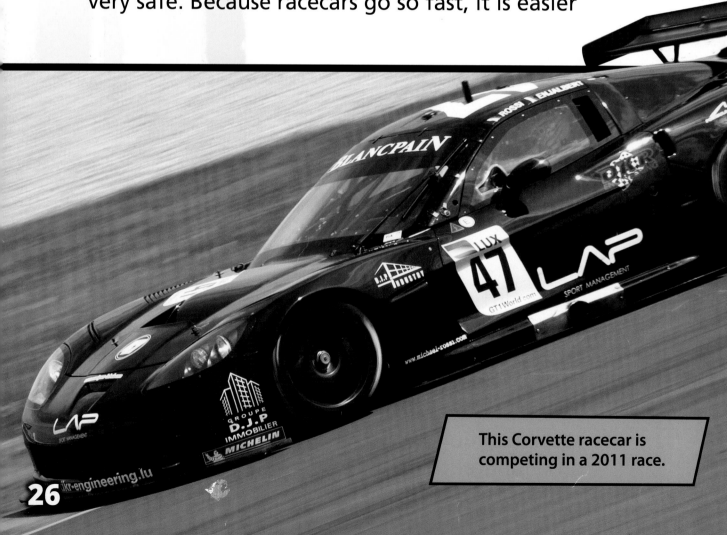

This Corvette racecar is competing in a 2011 race.

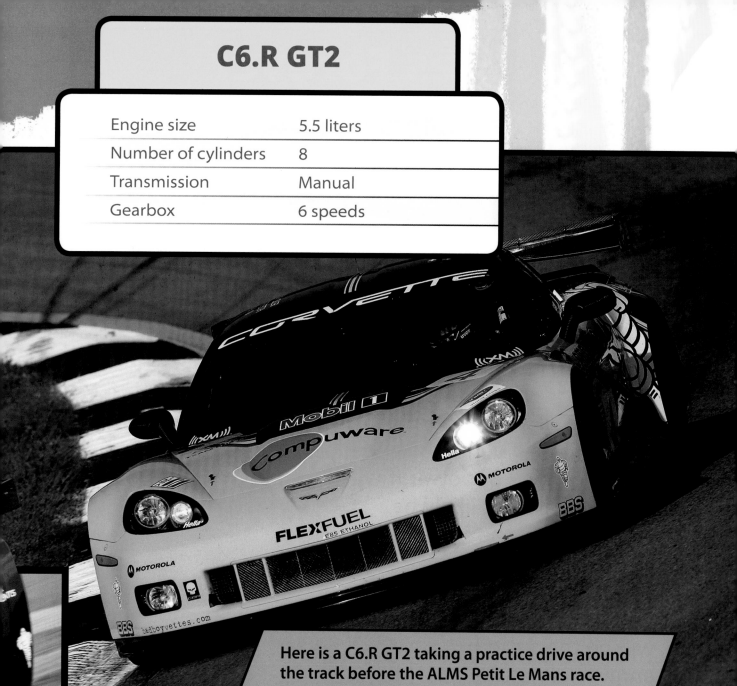

C6.R GT2

Engine size	5.5 liters
Number of cylinders	8
Transmission	Manual
Gearbox	6 speeds

Here is a C6.R GT2 taking a practice drive around the track before the ALMS Petit Le Mans race.

for them to crash. The GT2 has a cage that goes around the driver. This is so that if the car crashes, the driver will not be crushed.

The C6.R GT2 competes against European racecars in GT2 races. Ferrari, Porsche, Aston Martin, and many cars race in the ALMS with the C6.R GT2.

Corvettes Forever

The Corvette is one of the oldest American sports cars. Corvettes have managed to remain successful and popular by always using innovative technology and having designs that become classics.

As of 2012, Chevrolet is working on the seventh generation of Corvette, which will be known as C7. General Motors has been very secretive about what this new generation will look like and what kind of power it will have. It will most likely be introduced in the fall of 2013. Experts in the car industry think this is likely because 2013 will be the sixtieth anniversary of the Corvette, which makes it a good time to make an exciting announcement about Corvettes. The new generation will probably be pretty similar in appearance to the sixth generation but with an even more powerful engine. This will remind people that the Corvette is a car with history that will also be a car of the future.

Here is a Corvette concept model car. A concept car shows ideas that a carmaker is working on and may produce one day.

Comparing Corvettes

CAR	YEARS MADE	NUMBER PRODUCED	TOP SPEED	FACT
1957 Corvette	1957	6,339	132 mph (212 km/h)	Because this was the first year fuel-injected engines were available, only 1,040 were made with this option.
1963 Sting Ray	1963	21,513	132 mph (212 km/h)	This was the first Corvette to have independent rear suspension.
1968 Stingray	1968	28,566	128 mph (206 km/h)	This third-generation Corvette was designed after Chevrolet's Mako Shark II concept model.
1997 Corvette	1997	9,752	172 mph (277 km/h)	Production started late on this model, so very few were made compared to other models.
2012 ZR1	2011–	129	205 mph (330 km/h)	Achieved the fastest recorded speed for a production car on the Bonneville Salt Flats.

Glossary

accelerates (ik-SEH-luh-rayts) Increases in speed.

aerodynamic (er-oh-dy-NA-mik) Made to move through the air easily.

affordable (uh-FOR-duh-bul) Low enough in price to be bought by many people.

carburetor (KAHR-buh-ray-tur) A part in a car that mixes fuel and air correctly for an internal combustion engine.

compete (kum-PEET) To oppose another in a game or test.

cylinders (SIH-len-derz) The enclosed spaces for pistons in an engine.

division (dih-VIH-zhun) A group or department.

environment (en-VY-ern-ment) Everything that surrounds human beings and other organisms and everything that makes it possible for them to live.

fuel-injected (fyool-in-JEKT-ed) Having to do with a system that puts an exact amount of fuel into an internal combustion engine.

horsepower (HORS-pow-er) The way an engine's power is measured. One horsepower is the power to lift 550 pounds (250 kg) 1 foot (.3 m) in 1 second.

innovation (ih-nuh-VAY-shun) The creation of something new.

modernized (MO-der-nyzd) Made up-to-date.

produced (pruh-DOOSD) Made something.

production (pruh-DUK-shun) In the process of being made.

symbolic (sim-BAH-lik) Standing for something else.

transmission (trans-MIH-shun) A group of parts that includes the gears for changing speeds and that conveys the power from the engine to the machine's rear wheel.

Index

Websites

Due to the changing nature of Internet links, PowerKids Press has developed an online list of websites related to the subject of this book. This site is updated regularly. Please use this link to access the list: www.powerkidslinks.com/smach/corv/